Get Healthy FAST with the Alkaline Diet

Lose Weight, Increase Energy and Kick Ass with Alkalinity

Copyright

All Information in this book is copyright to C.K. Media Enterprises, L.L.C. and Developed Life Books and may not be copied from, reproduced or sold without prior written permission.

Disclaimer

The information contained in this book is provided for general information and entertainment purposes only and **does not constitute medical, psychiatric, legal or other professional advice on any subject matter**. The author of this book **is not a doctor and make no claims to be one** and does not accept any responsibility for any loss which may arise from reliance on information contained within this book or on any associated websites or blogs. The author of this book is NOT a licensed therapist and makes no claims to be. To read from here onward, it is assumed the reader has taken the diligence to read this message

The "Fire Lotus" Seal of Quality

DevelopedLife.com prides itself on high-quality content. We are against the trend on Amazon / Kindle of cheap, outsourced content written by non-authors.

Free Supplemental Booklet: Right now you can check out www.developedlife.com/subscribe and receive a free copy of the booklet **"10 Success Techniques to Master Your Life"** for those who desire to create optimal life philosophies. This is an important resource to have alongside this book.

You can also visit the exclusive mailing list for natural health and wellness by going to www.developedlife.com/andreasilver, where you can stay in contact with Andrea personally, and get another cool free book: **"The 20 Most Deceptive Health Foods"**.

Contents

- Disclaimer 1
- How Alkalinity Works 6
  - The Role of pH Levels 7
  - Research by Gerry Schwalfenberg 7
  - The Rise of Acidity 9
  - Balancing the Alkalinity 14
  - How to Create Your Alkaline Diet 18
  - Alkaline and Weight Loss 22
  - What to Expect 23
- BREAKFAST 24
  - Vegan Pancakes 24
  - Refreshing Green Smoothie 25
  - Cinnamon Flavored Quinoa 26
  - Tangy Bruchestta 27
  - Fruity Porridge 28
  - Thaalipeth 29
  - Faux Sausage 30
  - Breakfast bread 31
  - Healthy Cereal 32
  - Faux Oatmeal 33
- LUNCH 35
  - Veggie Concoction 35
  - Broccoli Blast 37
  - Power-Packed Lunch 38
  - Quinoa Punch 39

Alkaline Diet Recipes

- Wrapped Falafel 40
- Rice Ripple 41
- Saucy Chickpea 42
- Stuffed Squash 43
- Quinoa Croquettes 44
- Sprouted Wrap 45

DINNER 46
- Marrow Mania 46
- Broccoli-Potatoes Combo 47
- Broccoli Infusion 48
- Spiced Up Cauliflower 49
- Thai Coconut Curry 50
- Tofu "Chicken" Nuggets 51
- Veggie Curry 52
- Spicy Lentil 53
- Basic Brussels Sprouts 54
- Zucchini Pasta 55
- Green Lasagna 56

DESSERT 57
- Cinnamon Flavored Ice-cream 57
- Fabulous Figs 59
- Lemony Pudding 60
- Blueberries Blast 61
- Peach Pie 62
- Green Pumpkin Pie 63
- Coco-Orange Delight 64
- Wholesome Cookie 65

- Date Dazzle 66
- Yummy Yam 67
- Blissful Vanilla 68
- Fruity Crumble 69
- Delicious Bread Pudding 70
- Lemongrass Legacy 71
- Fruit filled Flatbread 72
- Banana Pie 73
- Minty Pudding 74
- Manic Mousse 75
- Chocolate Pudding 75

Final Thoughts 77
- A Message from Andrea 77

How Alkalinity Works

Welcome! Thank you for your purchase of this book. Together, we are going to explore the potential of alkaline dieting, why it's become a fixture in my own lifestyle, and how you can use this amazing concept to **turn your life around and experience rapid healthy effects**.

I've tried out many diets before. Focusing on an increase of alkalinity is, to me, one of the most well-rounded of them all. By its nature, this diet is going to greatly increase your vitamins, nutrients, folic acid, and so forth. You'll be eating lots of great veggies, peppers, and other healthy additions. However, you are also eating these foods with a new purpose; to increase alkalinity levels, balancing your body's pH and obtaining optimal health.

As the title of this book states, I want you to **get healthy *fast*,** and this is done in two steps: overhauling your diet and increasing physical fitness levels.

This book is focused on the former. There are various ways to implement a new diet into your life, and alkalinity is just one strategy, **however it's a strategy I greatly suggest** as there are very interesting studies about how alkalinity improves various aspects of your physiological condition.

Some of the results that have been reported from this type of diet have included:

- A decreased risk of various diseases, including certain cancers
- Weight loss
- Improved mood
- Reduced inflammation
- Greater energy levels

Let's start exploring what alkalinity is all about:

The Role of pH Levels

pH is the abbreviation for potential hydrogen. The pH of any solution is the measure of its hydrogen ion concentration. The more oxygen and alkaline a fluid is, the higher the pH reading. The lower the pH reading, the more acidic and oxygen deprived the solution is. The pH scale ranges from 0 to 14. 7 is the neutral state and anything above is alkaline, below is acidic.

Too much alkalinity or acidity are both poisonous. The body / blood must remained right around a neutral to slightly alkaline level, which is about 7.4 on the pH scale. If it drops much below this (becomes acidic) or gains too much (becomes basic), it means there is some type of disease going on. If the chart changes too severely, cells start to die, and the body shuts down (you die).

Of course, this is the pH levels of our functioning organs and bloodstream; but some parts of the body may vary greatly. For an example, the stomach contains powerful extremely acidic conditions. The mouth and saliva may also change to acidic conditions depending on food that's just been eaten, or in the presence of a condition like acid reflux.

However, for the rest of your functioning body, the 7.4-7.5 levels are very important. This is your mildly alkaline baseline, and if your body begins to dip into acidic conditions, various health compromises can occur.

Research by Gerry Schwalfenberg

According to a journal published in 2011 out of the University of Alberta by Dr. Schwalfenberg, the healthful effects of alkalinity have been confirmed[1]. Schwalfenberg begins his research by attributing dropping pH levels all over the planet as related to many ecological concerns aside from just the negative health effects in humans.

The reason for this is industrialization. As ecological disasters occur, they correlate to acidity. Increased CO_2 deposition has resulted in a slight acidic increase to the world's oceans, which could spell catastrophic effects, such as the destruction of coral reefs. Schwalfenberg stresses that many of the world's environmental problems can be identified by observing lower pH levels. For instance, if an area of the ocean suffers from a chemical leak like an oil spill, the ocean is likely to increase in acidity, and this is the effect that could kill smaller organisms, disrupting the food chain, and causing species to go extinct.

The next issue is, of course, the pH levels of the human body. Fundamentally, our diets have become more acidic since our hunter gatherer (ie paleo) days. Since we started refining grains in the form of white breads at the beginning of agriculture, and then as we began to industrialize our food more recently with the addition of chemicals, preservatives, chlorides, etc—we have become much more acidic as a result of modern food. This could therefore be attributed to many diseases that we wouldn't have been at risk for earlier in history.

Upon his review of alkaline literature, Schwalfenberg makes some conclusions:

- Increased alkalinity, in the form of an increase in the right fruits and vegetables, should improve factors like bone health, reduce muscle wasting, reduce the presence of chronic conditions like hypertension, and overall decrease the risk of strokes.

---

[1] http://www.ncbi.nlm.nih.gov/pmc/articles/PMC3195546/

- Certain natural growth hormones are increased through an improved endocrine system. This results in improved cardiovascular health, memory, and cognition.

- Magnesium, which activates vitamin D, is increased through alkaline dieting, which then results in the many improved functions of the body and a further reduction of diseases.

- Alkalinity also assists cancer patients.

Finally, Schwalfenberg stresses to ensure proper soil used to grow crops. A poor, acidic soil could translate into fruits and vegetables that are inferior compared to healthy soil counterparts, which is a good reason to seek out farmer's markets and locally grown produce when you can. If the pH level of soil enters the 5s, it's considered quite acidic and this could be problematic for your food.

Schwalfenberg's research is important because he has made the effort to comb through dozens of other journals dating back the last couple of decades that relate to health and alkalinity. There's been a fair amount of back and forth debate about if alkalinity is an effective dietary strategy or not, but it's now much harder to discount the importance of this diet.

Aside from Schwalfenberg's reporting, there is a lot of other research out there about how high alkalinity levels can decrease tumor growth, reduce weight, improve your body's metabolism, increase energy, and even reduce free radical damage—leading to anti-aging effects.

The Rise of Acidity

Western diets are very high in the acidic range. Some speculate that it could be one of the reasons that cancer is so prevalent in the 21st century. Regardless of whether this is true or not, we do know that an acidic body is not healthy.

As we delve into the alkaline diet, one of the first things we need to do is identify what types of food to avoid due to high acidic content.

Alcohol

Although red wine is healthy for you in certain ways, all forms of alcohol should be taken in moderation, and one of many reasons is that they are high in acid content. Some wines have pH levels that approach 3.5. If alcohol is a regular part of your diet, you may be turning your body into an acidic nature.

Artificial Sweeteners

Aspartame, Sucralose etc are unanimously considered by most health experts to be deceptive wastes. Aside from other issues, including potential neurological problems caused by aspartame, these chemicals are also acidic in nature. Watch out!

Animal Meat

Going on an alkaline diet also means cutting out meat. Almost all animal proteins are acidic. The acidity is compounded when animal protein is fried in even more acidic oils or paired with white pastas.

Bananas

May be included in recipes as a tasty filler, but don't just snack on bananas by themselves, as they are high in acid content and relatively low in other nutrients compared to other fruits

Berries

Some berries tend to be more acidic in nature, such as raspberries and blueberries. Other fruits considered acidic are currents, plumes and prunes.

Black Tea

As with coffee, it's extremely acidic. If you love to drink black teas, make sure it's counter-balanced with plenty of alkalizing food.

Certain Nuts

Some nuts can be combined into alkaline recipes and it won't cause any harm. However, snacking on a lot of nuts—especially salty nuts—by themselves can lower your pH level. This includes cashews, peanuts, and almonds.

Chocolate

A hard one to give up. Chocolate is quite acidic in all its. The cheap processed milk chocolates probably moreso than rawer dark chocolates and cacao. The best strategy for this one is to just keep the rest of your diet balanced to a higher level of alkalinity so you can still enjoy chocolate or include it in your recipes.

Coffee

OK, I know the media constantly shifts in-between coffee being good for you and coffee being bad for you. One week it cures cancer, the next week it causes heart disease. The truth is that coffee won't kill you, but it is very acidic. One cup won't be a big deal, but if it's part of your regular diet, it's a problem.

Cooking Oils

Common cooking oils (the cheap ones) like corn and sunflower tend to be quite acidic in nature.

Corn

Kind of an "empty" vegetable; high in starch and sugar and not much else. Corn is also acidic, so it would be wise to limit it, or cut it out entirely from your diet.

Most Dairy

Most milk and cheese products range from either slightly acidic or neutral (cream, yogurt, etc) to highly acidic. As one example, parmesan cheese is much more acid forming than other cheeses with a very high acid renal load. In addition, American pasteurized cheeses usually have pH levels around 5—significantly more acidic than other cheeses.

Processed Sugary Crap

Corn syrups, molasses, processed unnatural honey—these are all tickets to an acidic body. You have to start eliminating them ASAP.

Soft Drinks

There's 101 reasons to give up soft drinks (sodas). Yet another reason is because they are very acidic. If you are going into the alkaline diet, cut out soft drinks, carbonated syrup drinks, and any similar drink completely out of your diet. **Coca Cola has a staggering pH level of 2. This stuff is pure acid!**

Sodium

Aside from raising blood pressure, very salty foods also raise your acidity. Try to limit salt in your recipes and definitely don't sit around snacking on salty chips or nuts. On the same note, be careful of salty sauces and dressings. For an example, soy sauce.

Sweets and Desserts

Candy bars, caramel, junk food, you're asking for trouble! There are many reasons, from the saturated fat to the high fructose corn syrup, to avoid junk food. In addition, they are also very acidic.

White Bread and Most Grains

White bread actually has a pH of 5, which is very acidic. This also includes white pastas and other simple carbs. There are many other reasons to avoid these, as well—including weight gain, and how they spike your blood with sudden sugar rushes following by those inevitable crashes where your energy levels drop. Subsequent sugar crashes also spike your hunger, making it a dieter's nightmare.

In addition to white bread, most grains in general are acidic, which is why a proper alkaline diet limits grains. However, you don't have to completely cut them out. Certain cereal grains, especially ones loaded with healthy nuts and seeds, can and should still be eaten.

Note that there's an entire line of thought that suggests we should cut out *all grains* from our diets. I don't really combine this philosophy into this cookbook because the alkaline diet is already 95% vegan, cutting out grains too would start to limit our food options too much for comfort. However, it *can* be done nutritiously if you are disciplined (please see my *Raw Food Diet* books).

White Processed Vinegar

Vinegar is supposed to be alkaline, however white processed cheap vinegars are quite acidic and should be avoided.

Other Sources:

Besides food, there are other ways to unintentionally acidify yourself.

Alkaline Diet Recipes

One is through medications. Taking a lot of aspirin regularly will keep your pH low. This doesn't mean that you should forego aspirin, especially if it's part of a health curriculum to prevent heart problems, However, if your aspirin taking is optional, it might be best to eliminate it.

Tobacco is also acid forming. Smoking cigarettes has plenty of bad effects, least of all acidifying your body.

Exposure to certain chemicals, like herbicides, could also acidify you. However, there is a lack of research to cite in relation to this. (You probably shouldn't exposing yourself to *Round Up* anyways).

Debatable:

Some products are debatable about whether they are acidic or alkaline. For instance, mustard is often listed as both. As is vinegar.

Typically, the reasons for this include food processing or chemical additives that may turn something more acid. This is why white vinegar is more acidic compared to an organic brand of Balsamic or cider vinegar that could be alkaline. Another example is mustard. Common store bought yellow mustard is going to be more acidic than some good horseradish or Dion mustard that will be fairly alkaline.

Balancing the Alkalinity

And now let's take a look at the types of food that will take a bite out of your body's high acid levels.

Alkaline Fruits

While some fruits are a bit acidic (tomatoes), others are very alkaline in nature. The ones to think about are: *mango, melons, papaya, cantaloupe, kiwi, apricots, apples, ripe bananas, dates, ripe bananas, watermelons* and certain berries (acai is a good one).

A few of these fruits are especially noteworthy. For instance, a watermelon has a pH level of 9, and also acts as an excellent cleanser. You can further drink watermelon juice by itself as a thirst quencher which will also alkalize you.

"Acid" Fruit

When you think of alkalinity, do you think of limes and lemons? Conventional wisdom may suggest these are acidic, but no! They're "kings" of alkalinity. A lemon's pH level is massively alkaline at 9.0. Although lemon juice acts as an acidic compound, it's really electrolytic. Lemon juice can, for instance, balance out a person's pH level if suffering from heartburn from stomach acid. Consider keeping lemons on hand for most of the recipes in this book. If it works for that type of meal, sprinkle some lemon on it to further increase alkalinity levels.

Cinnamon

Cinnamon comes from the bark of the evergreen cinnamon tree. It has many purposes for flavoring, and it's one of the most alkaline spices. You'll find cinnamon included in many of the later recipes to provide kicks of alkalinity. In addition, as I talk about in my book *Natural Weight Loss Hacks and Secrets Revealed*, cinnamon is an interesting ingredient because it's one of the foods that boosts your metabolism. A faster metabolism means

Coconut

You'll find coconut ingredients listed often as an all-purpose alkalizing treat. The best thing about coconut is its myriad of uses. The oil can be cooked with, the meat is a natural vegetarian source of protein, and the milk can be used in substitution of regular milk for vegan recipes.

Curry

Popular spice across Asia. Curry works in numerous dishes. You can buy it powdered and make specialty sauces.

Garlic

Very alkaline and very good for you for many other reasons. One of the best ways to enjoy garlic is to simply roast a clove in half in the oven at 400 F for 15-20 minutes. The caramelized garlic tastes sweet and can even be used as a spread.

Mushrooms

Mushrooms like Japanese Shiitake have been known to have an alkalizing effect.

Leafy Green Vegetables

One of the primary sources of alkalinity in this diet is going to come from leafy green veggies. The high level of alkalinity is the result of chlorophyll itself, which is an alkaline compound. The right "green stuff" in your diet also means an infusion of vitamins K, A, C, E, fiber, b2, magnesium, iron, folate, etc.

You should think about:

Asparagus: Named after asparagines, an amino acid that helps with brain function. This plant is unusually high in alkalinity.
Broccoli: Great tasting lightly boiled or raw. Highly alkaline.
Spinach: Easy to buy, great in tons of recipes. High amounts of every nutrient and also a good source of natural calcium.

Alkaline Diet Recipes

Kale: A "superfood" that I talk about at length in my anti-aging & natural weight loss books. No matter what diet you choose, whether this or another one, stock up on kale and try to eat it every-day. That alone will make a massive difference.

Avocado: Nature's supply of healthy fats, alkalinity, and nutrients. Mash a single avocado and put some lemon on it for an easy to make and great little treat. You can also use it for some imaginative recipes. You can even include it in pies, mixed with pumpkin, for a green pumpkin pie!

Peppers

You will find that many alkaline recipes are loaded, when possible, with peppers. This ranges from chili peppers to more common (and perhaps easier to eat) bell peppers of various kinds; including the green, red, yellow, and orange varieties. There are more health benefits of peppers, as well. Red, yellow and orange bells are loaded with carotenoids which are important for skin health and have been known to lessen the advancement of age.

Sea Salt

Although sodium is acidic, this relates in part to the chemical processing that regular table salt undergoes. By contrast, natural sea salt is actually more alkaline. This is very good to know, as some food just doesn't taste that good unsalted—so you can replace your regular table salt and processed sodium products as appropriate. The best source of alkaline salt would be pink Himalyan rock salt which you can find at most specialty grocery stores.

Tempeh and Tofu (fermented)

These protein rich foods are standard fare in the East. As we are cutting out animal proteins in this diet, it's important to find appropriate substitutions, as every day you need to consume protein. While coconut meat is a good source, you need a variety—

nd ...k up at your local Asian grocer with fermented ...tly fry tofu in some coconut oil for a tasty protein

s

...atoes are higher in acid content than most other fruits. This ...oesn't mean you cannot eat them. They should be included as part of a recipe with other alkaline foods. In other words, sprinkling some lemon juice on tomatoes is a nice alkaline snack. They alkalize in a similar way as lemons. Despite being "high acid" their pH levels are also very high, making them basic.

How to Create Your Alkaline Diet

Now that we understand the foods that promote or demote alkalinity, let's explore the fundamentals of how to prepare an alkaline diet for yourself.

60% - 40 % Rule

The guideline for an alkaline diet is to make sure 60% of the foods you eat fall into the alkaline list. This could be attributed to a single recipe, as well. So if you're preparing a meal of 60% green veggies and 40% red meat, it's still a dish that's more alkalizing than not.

Of course, to reap the benefits of an alkaline diet you should seek to increase the alkalinity ratio by a higher margin, especially at first. After maybe a month of making this more into a 90% - 10 % ratio, you can reintroduce more acidic foods into your diet. This is to give your body a stronger dose of alkalinity if you're recovering from years of overly acidic eating.

So, You Don't Have to Give Everything Up...

That's the good thing about alkaline diets is that you don't have to swear off your favorite foods forever. If you eat mostly alkaline foods all day, and then you have a white bread peanut butter and jelly sandwich—it's not going to kill you. The big picture is not individual meals but your overall dietary trends over the long-term.

Watch Out for the Major Acid Promoters

You need to be strict when it comes to the major culprits that have resulted in an overly-acidified culture.

The biggest culprit is coffee. This is surprisingly hard to kick, and you know something's not right in your body when you find yourself unable to give up any type of substance due to addiction. Sadly, caffeine is addictive, and if you guzzle six cups a day you'll find it's not easy to keep your hands off the espresso machine. In addition to coffee, black teas are also acidic.

The obvious solution to the coffee dilemma is green tea. Green teas often contain the caffeine you're craving, but without the acidic effects. In addition, the caffeine dose is milder so it's also a good way to kick your addiction to the heavier doses in regular coffees. Green tea is mildly alkaline in nature, and not acidic at all.

Some may be reading this and looking for the closest pitchfork—as they're that defensive about their coffee routine. Understand one thing: with the 60/40 rule, you can still drink coffee on an alkaline diet, *but you can't drink six cups a day*. You can drink two cups and ensure you have alkaline meals consistently.

The next major acid promoter is refined white sugar and junk foods of every variety. This includes foods like top ramen, which are highly refined and contain no nutritional benefits. It's important to work hard to eliminate these types of foods from your diet.

Next is tobacco. This is not a book about giving up smoking, and I've personally never smoked so I cannot offer much advice in this regard. However, it's something you need to start seriously thinking about. While an alkaline diet may counter some of the acidifying effects of cigarette smoke, you're still handicapping yourself if you begin this diet without first giving up smoking.

The final major culprit are drugs. The USA is perhaps the most medicated culture in the world. Many pharmaceuticals are *highly* acidic in nature. When you are popping six or seven different tablets a day, it's a big problem.

I always recommend the same advice when it comes to pharmaceuticals: figure out a strategy to kick the ones that aren't immediately important for your health. A prescription sleep aid like *Ambien*, for instance, can be replaced with a combination of herbal supplements and psychological practices like meditation. I am 100% convinced that insomnia is not something we need to take hard chemicals to cure.

The same can be said for psychiatric drugs in *most* circumstances. However, this is a hard subject to tackle. Many people become dependent on these things and cannot simply go cold turkey. Instead, you must try to wean yourself off them. If you have a doctor who believes you should *permanently* be on anti-depressants, then you need to find yourself a new doctor, one who is not a zombie of big pharma.

The proper strategy is to practice psychological therapies to fix your emotional / mood disorders. Drugs that boost your serotonin levels and other "happy" chemicals in your brain are really designed to be temporary band-aids to help a patient learn to maintain their emotions on their own. It's the prerogative of the manufacturers to market their pills as permanent solutions, which was never their intended purpose.

This is an area of health that requires a lot of vigilance.

Organic and Healthy

Every food you pick should be done thoughtfully. Unfortunately, this is hard because these days "organic" is simply used as a sales strategy. A company may slap an organic label on something and expect consumers to buy it with no questions asked.

Another issue is that the organic strategy in question gives companies a reason to justify jacking the price up tenfold. Many complain, rightfully how it's hard to eat healthy because of the price difference.

There's no easy solution for these problems. The first is to be mindful of the *ingredients* list more than the label. It could say organic, but if it's loaded with far too many ingredients than what it should contain, it's probably filled with a high number of preservatives and other chemicals.

The next issue is a financial one. What can you sacrifice to eat better? If it costs an extra $100 per month to increase the nutritious content of your food, what other expenses can you eliminate to prioritize your health?

Time to Cook

One last important part of this diet (and any diet) is taking the time out to cook for yourself. With things like jobs, kids, and other responsibilities, how does one do this?

There's no easy answer. As someone who works from home, it's not as hard for me. But if I had to commute to work, I'd be tempted to start skipping on my diet and opting for whatever the nearest fast food or cafeteria solution was.

One thing to keep in mind is the 60 / 40 rule. This means if you eat just one meal per day that's pure alkaline ingredients, this could make up for less than alkaline meals at other parts in the day. For instance, if you eat a breakfast full of greens and alkaline fruits, you can afford to eat less alkaline meals for the rest of the day. However, when possible, always choose the leafy green vegetables. If your workplace or school has a cafeteria, load up on the broccoli and avoid that macaroni and cheese no matter how tempting it appears.

Alkaline and Weight Loss

At this point, you may be reading this and wondering about how this diet works in regard to weight loss. The answer is that it works great for losing weight. There are many other facets of this diet rolled into one. From giving up white pasta to eliminating sodas and junk foods and increasing good fats, the alkaline diet is as good as any diet is going to get.

In addition, some of these alkaline foods are excellent for keeping your metabolism working fast. This means more calories burned.

However, like any diet, simply changing what you eat is only half the battle. The other half involves regular physical exercise. As I mention frequently, my favorite form of exercise for weight loss is anaerobic—weight lifting and using machines. This burns calories fast without having to waste the entire day on a treadmill.

I also immediately lost many pounds the day I moved to a house on a hill, with the major stores about a mile beneath me. The hike uphill with a grocery bag or two every couple of days did wonders. The big point, however, is to avoid leading a sedentary lifestyle by whatever means possible.

You can't have one without the other. You can't diet without exercise and expect to lose a lot of weight. And you can't exercise without watching what you eat and expect many results, either.

Finally, I highly suggest to approach the alkaline dieting concept as a *lifestyle* and not so much a "diet". Just using the word diet, I've noticed, actually hinders the progress of many people (it's amazing the power that one's choice in words has).

By thinking of it as a lifestyle change, it's easier to stay committed to it. The more that you believe you are sacrificing greatly to perform something you wouldn't otherwise do, the more likely you'll fall of the wagon.

What to Expect

After a couple of weeks of following alkaline recipes, I hope you find yourself with increased energy, increased cognitive function (better memory, concentration, and problem solving), better complexion, and perhaps even the elimination of various ailments that you once thought you'd suffer from for the rest of your life.

As an example, alkaline dieting definitely improved / cured my acid reflux.

Everybody's bodies are different, however. I cannot say for sure what effects alkalizing will have on you, specifically. There are no absolutes or rules as they relate to a subject as complex as the human body. But one thing I can guarantee is that by following a diet like this one, you WILL become healthier, and if you are truly dedicated—you will become healthy FAST!

Let's get started:

BREAKFAST

Vegan Pancakes

Pancakes are a popular breakfast recipe that can be infused with some alkaline ingredients.

Serving Size: 6-8
Ingredients:

1. 1 cup **organic light spelt flour**
2. 2 tbsp **baking powder**
3. ⅛ tsp **fine Himalayan salt**
4. 1 cup **coconut milk**
5. 1 tbsp **agave maple syrup**
6. 2 tbsp **sunflower oil** (cold pressed)
7. 1 ½ **tsp vanilla**
8. ¼ Cup **coconut oil** (for cooking)

Procedure:
1. In a bowl, put all the ingredients except coconut oil, and blend well.
2. On a heated pan, drizzle coconut oil and pour the smooth batter in the shape of cakes. Let it cook until bubbles

appear for about 2-3 minutes. Flip it over and cook for another 1-2 minutes.
3. Serve with maple syrup.

Refreshing Green Smoothie

Refreshing green smoothie is a power packed boost of energy to keep you going all-day long.

Serving Size: 1
Ingredients:

1. 1 large **cucumber** (chopped)
2. 3 medium **Kale leaves** (shredded)
3. 5 stems **fresh mint** (chopped)
4. 3 stems **fresh parsley** (chopped)
5. 1 inch **fresh ginger** (chopped)
6. 1 **avocado** (chopped)
7. 1 cup **coconut water**
8. **fresh juice of one lime**
9. 1-2 tsp **udo's oil**
10. 1-2 tbsp **hemp seeds**
11. 2-3 drops **stevia**

Procedure:
1. Put all the ingredients in a blender to get a smooth consistency.
2. Pour it into a glass and serve.

Cinnamon Flavored Quinoa

Cinnamon Flavored Quinoa is an interesting variation of oatmeal. Recall that cinnamon has alkalizing effects.

Serving Size: 3-4
Ingredients:

1. 1 cup **quinoa** (rinsed and soaked)
2. 3 cups **coconut milk**
3. ½ tsp **vanilla**
4. 1 tsp **cinnamon** (powdered)
5. ¼ tsp **allspice** (powdered)
6. ½ cup **raisins** (soaked)
7. 1 medium-sized **apple** (chopped)
8. ¼ Cup **stevia**
9. ½ cup **walnuts** (chopped)
10. 4 tbsp **sunflower seeds**
11. 1 cup **blueberries** (chopped)

Procedure:
1. In a saucepan, combine all the ingredients except the fruits and nuts. Let it simmer on medium flame for about 6-8 minutes until the liquid is absorbed.
2. Remove from the flame and serve with chopped nuts and fruits.

Tangy Bruchestta

Tangy Bruchestta is a crunchy breakfast meal, and quite popular amongst the garlic bread fans.

Serving Size: 5-6
Ingredients:

1. 1 **spelt baguette** (thinly sliced)
2. 4 medium-sized **tomatoes** (diced)
3. 4 **garlic cloves** (crushed)
4. ¼ Cup **extra virgin olive oil**
5. 12 small **basil leaves** (shredded)
6. **Celtic Salt** to taste

Pesto
1. 1 cup **basil leaves** (shredded**)**
2. ½ c **raw organic almonds**
3. ⅓ c **extra virgin olive oil**
4. 1 large **garlic clove** (roughly chopped)
5. ¼ tsp **Celtic sea salt**

Procedure:
1. Toast the sliced baguette in an oven at a temperature of 400°F for roughly 10 minutes.
2. In the meantime, soak the crushed garlic cloves into olive oil and keep it aside for about 30 minutes or so. This would let the garlic flavor combine in the olive oil. In addition to this, generously sprinkle salt over tomatoes and keep it aside too.
3. To prepare pesto, combine all the ingredients mentioned in a food processor and blend.
4. Once done, remove from the oven and apply the garlic infused olive oil and pesto sauce. Place the tomatoes over it and garnish with basil leaf.

Fruity Porridge

Serving Size: 1
Ingredients:

1. 1 cup **filtered water**
2. ⅓ cup **thin flaked spelt**
3. **cinnamon** to taste
4. ¼ Cup **stevia**
5. ¼ tsp **vanilla extract**
6. 2-3 tbsp **cranberries** (dried)

Procedure:

1. In a heated pan, put all the ingredients and cook. Let the ingredients simmer for about 4-5 minutes until blended well.
2. Pour it into a serving bowl and serve with preferably non-dairy milk.

Thaalipeth

Thaalipeth is a healthy breakfast from India.

Serving Size: 1-2
Ingredients:

1. 1 cup **rajgira flour**
2. 1 cup **potatoes** (boiled and mashed)
3. 2 tbsp **coriander leaves** (chopped)
4. 1 tbsp **green chili** (paste)
5. 1 tbsp **cumin seeds** (crushed)
6. 1 tsp **sesame seeds**
7. 2 tbsp **peanut powder** (roasted)
8. Salt to taste

Procedure:

1. In a bowl, combine all ingredients into stiff dough. Once the dough is prepared, let it rest for 5 minutes.
2. Make small balls of the dough and roll them flat with the help of a rolling pin.
3. Place these flat breads on a dehydrator for about 5-6 hours.

Faux Sausage

Faux sausage is a healthy breakfast and snack that can be loaded with alkaline peppers.

Serving Size: 1
Ingredients:

1. **2 dates** (pitted and chopped)
2. ½ tsp **fennel seed**
3. 1 cup **walnuts** (chopped)
4. pinch of **cayenne**
5. ¼ Cup **red pepper** (crushed)
6. ¼ tsp **salt**
7. ¼ tsp **pepper**
8. ¼ tsp **oregano**
9. ¼ tsp **basil**

Procedure:

1. In a food processor, combine all the ingredients well.
2. Transfer this mix in a plate and make small balls.
3. Place them on a dehydrator tray for about 5-7 hours at a temperature of about 110° F.

Breakfast bread

Breakfast bread is a healthier version of the usual white or brown bread consumed for breakfast. Loaded with healthy doses of alkalinity in the form of peppers, onions and seeds.

Serving Size: 3-4
Ingredients:

1. 2 **whole onions chopped**
2. 1-2 **jalapenos peppers** (deseeded)
3. 3 Tbsp **sundried tomatoes** (soaked in oil)
4. ½ cup **ground flax seed**
5. ¼ cup **ground chia seed**
6. ½ cup **sunflower seeds**
7. ½ cup **pumpkin seeds**
8. 2 tbsp **amino**

Procedure:
1. Combine all the ingredients in a food processor and spread it o a dehydrator.
2. Dehydrate for about 12 hours on each side before serving.

Alkaline Diet Recipes

Healthy Cereal

Healthy cereal combines the wholesome goodness of nuts and seeds put together.

Serving Size: 1-2
Ingredients:

1. ½ cup **sunflower seeds**
2. 1 ¼ cups **coconut milk** (soak almonds in milk overnight and blend)
3. ¼ cup **dry coconut** (dried and chopped)
4. ¼ cup **almonds** (soaked and chopped)
5. ¼ cup **pumpkin seeds** (soaked)
6. ½ cup **raisins** (soaked)
7. 6 **small dates** (pitted, soaked and chopped)
8. ¼ cup **chia seeds** (soaked in water)

Procedure:
1. In a blender, put all the ingredients except raisins, Blend coarsely.
2. In a bowl, pour the blended mix and raisins with dash of pounded cinnamon.
3. Serve immediately.

Faux Oatmeal

Faux oatmeal is an ideal breakfast recipe to start your day.

Serving Size: 1-2
Ingredients:

1. 3 **bananas** (sliced)
2. ¼ Cup **walnuts** (chopped)
3. ¼ Cup **coconut** (dried and chopped)
4. ⅛ Cup **cinnamon** (pounded)
5. ⅛ Cup **agave nectar**

Procedure:
1. In a bowl, mix all the ingredients and serve.

Hey! You reading this! Did you receive your _free_ gift yet?

I don't want you to get fooled anymore at the checkout aisle. That's why I've created a free e-book to reveal deceptive health foods that consumers need to beware of.

THE 20 MOST DECEPTIVE HEALTH FOODS

ANDREA SILVER

I'm giving it away right now for readers. You can get it at www.developedlife.com/andreasilver

LUNCH

Veggie Concoction

Veggie Concoction is a mix of different vegetables in one recipe, putting a big dose of alkalinity into your diet.

Serving Size: 2-3
Ingredients:

1. 2 Cups **Any Vegetable (chopped)**
2. 2 cups **water**
3. 3 **garlic cloves**
4. ½ cup **extra virgin olive oil**
5. 1 tsp **sea salt**
6. 2 - 3 tbsp **yellow curry powder**
7. 1 cup **almonds** (soaked)
8. ¼ cup **cilantro** (chopped)
9. ¼ cup **parsley** (chopped)

Procedure:
1. To prepare marinade, combine all the ingredients mentioned except vegetable in a food processor.

2. Once the marinade is prepared, generously rub into the vegetables. Keep it for about 1-2 hours.
3. Bake it in a preheated oven at a temperature of about 450° F.

Broccoli Blast

Broccoli blast is bursting with nutrients from countless sources. This is one recipe PACKED with alkaline power.

Serving Size:
Ingredients:

1. 1 **kale head** (chopped)
2. 1 cup **almond butter**
3. 2 **jalapeno peppers** (seeded and chopped)
4. 2 cups **broccoli heads** (chopped)
5. 1 cup **mint** (minced)
6. 1 cup **raisins**
7. 2 tsp **asafetida**
8. 1 tsp **tarragon**
9. 1 tbsp **coconut butter**
10. 1 tbsp **lime leaf (minced)**
11. 2 tbsp **lemongrass** (minced)
12. 1 bunch **dandelion leaves,** (shredded)
13. 1 tbsp **ginger**
14. 2 tsp **salt**
15. 1 cup **coconut water**

Procedure:
1. To prepare the marinade, blend all the ingredients except dandelion greens, kale and broccoli.
2. Once the marinade is prepared, toss the remaining ingredients well.
3. Put the dish in a dehydrator for about 4-5 hours at the lowest temperature.
4. Check the doneness and serve.

Power-Packed Lunch

As the title suggests. This is a varied lunch meal designed as a huge boost of energy.

Serving Size: 2-3
Ingredients:

Broccoli:
1. 1 **broccoli** (chopped)
2. ½ cup **tamari**
3. 1 Tsp **sea salt**
4. ½ cup **olive oil**

Pasta:
1. 2 cup **raw beetroot**
2. ¼ cup **olive oil**
3. 6 **courgettes**
4. 1Tsp **sea salt**

Walnut pesto:
1. 1 cup **walnuts** (chopped)
2. 2 cup **basil** (shredded)
3. 2 **lemon** (juice)
4. 2 tsp **sea salt**
5. ¼ cup **olive oil**

Procedure:
1. To prepare marinade for broccoli, mix all the ingredients mentioned. Toss broccoli in it and keep it aside.
2. For pasta, cut the courgette in linguine strips, and toss it with other ingredients mentioned.
3. Lastly, prepare a walnut pesto, by combining all the ingredients mentioned under it.
4. Place pasta on a serving plate and top it with broccoli and pesto sauce.

Quinoa Punch

Quinoa Punch combines a sumptuous mix of ingredients for a good lunch.

Serving Size: 4-5
Ingredients:

1. 4 cups **quinoa** (sprouted)
2. 4 green **onions** (thinly sliced)
3. 1 large **tomato** (seeded and diced)
4. ¾ **cucumber** (peeled, seeded and diced)
5. ¼ cup **parsley** (minced)
6. 20 mint **leaves** (minced)
7. 3-5 **lemon** (juice)
8. 1-2 tbsp **tamari**

Procedure:
1. In a bowl, mix all the ingredients and keep it aside for about an hour.
2. Serve with a dash of lemon.

Wrapped Falafel

Wrapped falafel is a bean-less delight in romaine lettuce.

Serving Size: 2-3
Ingredients:

Bean-less Falafel:
1. 2 cups **almonds**
2. ½ cup **cilantro**
3. 4 Tbsp **lemon juice**
4. 2 Tbsp **tahini**
5. ¼ cup **parsley**
6. 1 Tbsp **olive oil**
7. 1 ½ tsp **ground cumin**
8. 1 tsp **sea salt**
9. ¾ cup **water**

Cucumber Sauce:
1. ½ large **cucumber** (peeled, seeded and sliced)
2. ¼ cup **fresh dill weed** (shredded)
3. ½ **lemon** (juice)
4. 1 Tbsp **honey**
5. ¼ cup **raw tahini**
6. ¼ tsp **salt**

Procedure:
1. To prepare falafel, blend all the ingredients mentioned. Make small balls of the mix and dehydrate for about 4-5 hours at a temperature of 115° F.
2. In the meantime, prepare cucumber sauce by blending in all its ingredients.
3. To serve, roll up the falafel balls in romaine lettuce with a little bit of cucumber sauce.

Alkaline Diet Recipes

Rice Ripple

Rice Ripple offers a healthy alternative to rice-based recipes.

Serving Size: 2-3
Ingredients:

1. 1 whole **cauliflower** (grated)
2. 2 **Lemon** (juice)
3. ¼ Cup **sesame seeds**
4. 2 **Garlic cloves** (crushed)
5. 1 inch long **ginger** (crushed)
6. 6 tsp **namu shoya**
7. 4 tsp **raw honey**
8. ⅛ Cup **Himalayan salt**

Procedure:
1. Blend all the ingredients except cauliflower to prepare a sauce like paste.
2. The grated cauliflower acts as rice alternative.
3. To serve, put the cauliflower and top it with the sauce.

Saucy Chickpea

Saucy Chickpea is a delicious curried recipe that is nutritious too.

Serving Size: 2-3
Ingredients:

Sauce:
1. 1 medium **eggplant** (chopped)
2. 1 tbsp **curry powder**
3. ¼ Cup **Cayenne pepper**
4. 1 **garlic clove** (crushed)
5. 1 tsp **cumin seeds**
6. ½ cup **water**
7. 1 tsp **salt**

Dish:
1. 1 cup **dried chickpeas,** (soaked overnight)
2. 1 cup **broccoli** (chopped)
3. 1 Cup **cauliflower** (chopped)
4. 2 medium **tomatoes** (chopped)
5. 1 tbsp **olive oil**

Procedure:
1. Prepare a sauce by combining all the ingredients mentioned.
2. In a heated pan, sauté onions and chickpea. To this, add other vegetables and ingredients. Cook for 10 minutes.
3. Pour in the sauce and cook until blends well. Let it simmer for about 10-15 minutes.
4. Serve with pita bread.

Stuffed Squash

Squash filled with nuts, quinoa, raisins, etc. Really healthy, really tasty!

Serving Size: 5-6
Ingredients:
1. 4-6 pale **yellow summer squash** (peeled, halved and seeded)
2. ½ cup **sunflower seeds** (soaked)
3. ½ cup **quinoa** (uncooked)
4. ¼ cup **raisins** (soaked)
5. ¼ Cup **olive oil**
6. ¼ Cup **nama shoyu**

Procedure:
1. Coat the squash halves with a mix of olive oil and nama shoyu.
2. I a bowl mix all the remaining ingredients for stuffing. With the help of a spoon, fill the stuffing in the squash.
3. Dehydrate for about 5-6 hours at a temperature of 115° F.

Quinoa Croquettes

Quinoa Croquettes is a mouth-watering recipe that is ideal for parties and celebrations.

Serving Size: 7-8
Ingredients:

1. 1 cup **dry quinoa** (cooked in 2 cups water)
2. 1 Cup **pinto beans** (boiled, drained and rinsed)
3. 1 very **large sweet potato** (peeled, diced, steamed, mashed)
4. 1 tsp **Celtic sea salt**
5. 1 cup **Onion** (finely diced)
6. 4 **garlic cloves** (crushed)
7. 3 tbsp **olive oil**
8. ½ cup **red pepper** (finely diced)
9. ⅓ cup **fresh cilantro** (chopped)
10. ½ cup **hemp seeds**
11. 1 tsp **dried oregano** (dried)
12. 1 tsp **ground cumin**
13. 1 Lemon **(juice)**

Procedure:
1. In a pan sauté onions, crushed garlic and red pepper. To this add, other ingredients. Once blended well. Remove from flame and let it cool.
2. Make croquettes from the mixture, and put in the heated pan. Flip them over so that it is brown on both sides.

Sprouted Wrap

Sprouted Wrap is combination of vegetables and lentils wrapped in a tortilla wrap.

Serving Size: 4-6
Ingredients:

1. 1 **parsnip** (peeled and diced)
2. 4-6 **sprouted grain tortilla wraps**
3. 1 large **sweet potato** (peeled and diced)
4. 1 **yellow beet** (peeled and diced)
5. 3-4 tbsp **olive oil**
6. 1 tsp **sea salt**
7. 2 **medium beets** (peeled and diced)
8. 1 Cup **mixed greens**
9. ½ Cup **fresh pea shoots**

Procedure:
1. Blend all the ingredients in a processor except mixed green and tortilla wraps.
2. Spread this over the dehydrator tray. Dehydrate for about 25-30 minutes at 375° F.
3. Place these dehydrated spreads on the tortilla wraps along with mixed greens and serve.

DINNER

Marrow Mania

Marrow Mania is an interesting marrow rich recipe good for alkaline dieters.

Serving Size: 1-2

Ingredients:
1. 1 large **marrows** (cut into rings)
2. 1 large **onion** (chopped)
3. 3 **bread slices**
4. 3-4 tbsp **olive oil** (for coating)
5. 2 tsp **fresh basil** (shredded)
6. 1 cup **almonds** (soaked)

Procedure:
1. In a food processor, blend all the ingredients except marrow to a paste-like consistency.
2. Marinade the marrow rings in this blend.
3. Bake the marinated rings in a preheated oven at a temperature of 380°F for about an hour or until golden.

4. Remove from the oven and serve with cilantro garnish.

Broccoli-Potatoes Combo

Broccoli-Potato Combo is a unique blend of green vegetable with high carbohydrate content potato.

Serving Size: 3-4
Ingredients:

1. 2 large **Onions** (diced)
2. 4-6 **Garlic cloves** (crushed)
3. 3-4 **Potatoes** (chopped)
4. 1 tbsp **Oregano** (dry)
5. **Cayenne Pepper** to taste
6. 1 **Broccoli** (chopped)
7. 1 ½ **Cup Tomatoes** (crushed with basil)

Procedure:
1. Mix and place all the ingredients except broccoli, tomatoes, and potatoes. Let them cook on high temperature for about 5- 7 Minutes. To this, add potatoes, and continue cooking for 10 minutes.
2. Once the potatoes are done, place broccoli and tomatoes. Cook for about 15-20 minutes until, all the ingredients blend in well.
3. Serve warm.

Broccoli Infusion

Broccoli Infusion is an interesting recipe that makes for extremely good tasting and alkaline enriched broccoli.

Serving Size: 1-2
Ingredients:

1. 1 **broccoli head**
2. ¼ cup **olive oil**
3. 1 tsp **nama shoyu**
4. 1 tsp **apple cider vinegar**
5. ¼ Cup **sea salt**

Procedure:
1. In a bowl mix all the ingredients except broccoli. Mix them well and toss broccoli with it.
2. Keep it marinated for about 4-6 hours, and bake for about 5-10 minutes.
3. Serve warm.

Spiced Up Cauliflower

Spiced Up Cauliflower is full of flavor, making it an excellent main dish or a side course.

Serving Size: 2-3
Ingredients:

1. 1 head **cauliflower** (chopped)
2. 1 cup **brazil nuts** (chopped)
3. ¼ cup **olive oil**
4. 1 **lemon** (juice)
5. 3 tsp **garam masala**
6. pinch of **cayenne**

Procedure:
1. In a bowl, blend, all the ingredients except cauliflower.
2. Once the ingredients are mixed well, toss the cauliflower into it.
3. Dehydrate the marinated cauliflower for about 1-2 hours.
4. Serve with cilantro garnish.

Thai Coconut Curry

Thai Coconut Curry is an alternative recipe of the rich Thai dish. Jalapenos or regular Thai hot peppers can work for this dish to spice it up. If you don't like very hot foods then replace it with non-hot chili or bell peppers.

Serving Size: 2-3
Ingredients:

1. ¾ cup **fresh young coconut meat**
2. 3 **jalapenos** (seeded and chopped)
3. 1 ½ tbsp **curry paste**
4. 1 cup **almonds** (chopped)
5. 1 ½ **cup water**
6. 1 tbsp **sweetener**
7. 1 **basil leaf**
8. 1 tbsp **cilantro** (chopped)
9. 1 inch long **ginger**
10. 3 tbsp **lemongrass**
11. 1 cup **cilantro** (shredded)
12. 1 **lime** (peeled and sliced)
13. ¼ Cup **salt**

Procedure:

1. To prepare the curry, combine jalapeno and lemongrass. In addition to this, add lime, ginger and other remaining ingredients until a smooth consistency is prepared.
2. Serve with cilantro garnish.

Tofu "Chicken" Nuggets

Tofu coated in a tasty seed marinade and fried.

Serving Size: 2-3
Ingredients:

1. 1 ½ Cup **tofu** (diced in medium to large chunks)
1. 2 cup **walnuts** (soaked overnight)
2. **1 cup sunflower seeds** (soaked overnight)
3. 1 cup **sundried tomatoes** (soaked overnight)
4. **2 cup sunflower seeds** (soaked overnight)
5. 1-2 **orange** (juice)

Procedure:
1. In a food processor, blend all the ingredients except the tofu.
2. Transfer the mix in a bowl and marinade the tofu in the blend.
3. Dehydrate it for about 5-7 hours on each side in the fridge.
4. Fry lightly in oil for 5-10 minutes on each side until each nugget is browned. Serve with a dressing of choice.

Veggie Curry

Veggie Curry is a flavorful curried recipe that is simply delicious and can be combined with breads of your choice.

Serving Size: 2-3
Ingredients:

1. **1 large onion** (chopped)
2. 2 **garlic cloves** (crushed)
3. 2 ½ tbsp **curry powder**
4. 1 Cup **tomatoes** (diced)
5. 1 cube **vegetable bouillon**
6. 1 Cup **mixed vegetables** (chopped)
7. 1 ½ cups **water**
8. 2 tbsp **tomato** (paste)
9. **Salt** to taste
10. **Pepper** to taste
11. 2 tbsp **chopped fresh cilantro** (shredded)

Procedure:
1. In a heated pan, sauté onions. To this, garlic, curry powder and tomatoes. Continue to sauté for about 2-3 minutes.
2. Once lightly golden brown, add the remaining ingredients, and cook for about 25-30 minutes. Continue to cook until tender and cooked.
3. Garnish with chopped cilantro and serve.

Spicy Lentil

Spicy lentil is a perfect snack or main meal that is high in protein, high in alkalinity, and low in calories.

Serving Size: 2-3
Ingredients:

1. 2 cups **mung beans or lentils** (soaked overnight and sprouted)
2. 2-4 tbsp **freshly grated coconut** (grated)
3. 1 ½ tbsp **sesame oil**
4. 1-2tbsp **lemon** (juice)
5. ¼ tsp **garam masala**
6. ⅛tsp **brown mustard seeds**
7. ⅛tsp **ground cumin seeds**
8. ⅛tsp **Celtic sea salt**

Procedure:
1. In a bowl, toss all the ingredients and the sprouted lentils.
2. Serve with an extra dash of lemon juice.

Basic Brussels Sprouts

Brussels sprouts are high in nutrients, calcium, folic aid, and a fantastic meal to keep your alkalinity levels in check.

Serving Size: 1-2
Ingredients:

1. 1 Cup **Brussels sprouts** (stems trimmed and halved)
2. 1 tsp **salt**
3. 2-3 tbsp **olive oil**
4. ½ tsp **freshly ground black pepper**

Procedure:
1. In a bowl, mix all the ingredients and toss with Brussels sprouts.
2. Place it in preheated over at a temperature of 375 degrees F and roast for about 20-25 minutes until crispy.

Zucchini Pasta

Zucchini Pasta is a delicious and healthy competitor of the Italian recipe.

Serving Size: 1-2
Ingredients:

1. 1 **Zucchini** (thinly sliced)
2. 1 Cup **Cherry Tomatoes** (halved)
3. 1 Cup **Pea Pods** (chopped)
4. ¾ Cup **Mushrooms** (marinated in nami shoyu and oil for ½ hour)
5. 5 **Scallions** (sliced)
6. ½ Cup **Sundried tomatoes** (dried and chopped)
7. ½ Cup **Spinach Cheese Spread**
8. ¼ Cup **Water**
9. **Sea salt** to taste
10. **Pepper** to taste

Procedure:
1. Prepare sauce by mixing cheese spread and water. Keep it aside for further use.
2. Toss all the ingredients in the sauce.

Green Lasagna

Green Lasagna is a veggie version of the popular Italian recipe.

Serving Size: 1
Ingredients:

1. ½ **Zucchini** (thinly sliced)
2. 2 cups **spinach leaves** (shredded)
3. ½ cup **Marinara sauce**
4. ½ **ripe avocado** (mashed)

Procedure:
1. In a square or rectangular container, cover the bottom with roughly 2 tablespoon of Marinara Sauce and place the zucchini noodles over it. Spread Marinara sauce over it and place avocado over it.
2. Continue to follow the same layering process with the rest of the ingredients. Refrigerate in a sealed container.
3. Take it from the freezer a few minutes before serving.

DESSERT

Cinnamon Flavored Ice-cream

Cinnamon Flavored Ice-cream is a yummy treat for kids and adults alike.

Serving Size: 4-5
Ingredients:

For the Cinnamon Ice Cream:
1. 2 ½ cups **coconut water**
2. 1 ½ cups **young coconut pulp**
3. 3 tbsp **coconut oil**
4. 3 tbsp **coconut oil**
5. 3-4 tbsp **coconut nectar**
6. 8 drops **stevia**
7. 1 ½ tbsp **pure vanilla extract**
8. ¼ cup **chaga irish moss gel**
9. 2 tsp **ground cinnamon**
10. 3 tbsp **coconut oil**
11. ¼ tsp **freshly ground nutmeg**

Orange Ginger Crunch:
1. 3 tbsp **macadamia nuts** (chopped)
2. ½ cup **coconut** (shredded)
3. 3 drops **orange essential oil**
4. 1 tsp **fresh minced ginger (minced)**
5. 1 ½ tbsp **coconut oil** (melted)
6. ½ **orange** (zest)
7. 2 drops **stevia**
8. 2 tsp **coconut nectar**
9. Pinch of **Himalayan salt**

Procedure:
1. To prepare Cinnamon Ice Cream, blend all the ingredients mentioned except oil. Blend the oil later. Refrigerate the mix for about 5-7 hours. Once semi-set, process it again in a blender and refrigerate for 4-5 hours.
2. Prepare the orange ginger crunch by blending all the ingredients together. Refrigerate the mix on a plate. Once set, break up in chinks for future use in the recipe.
3. To serve, scoop ice cream and top it with ginger crunch.

Fabulous Figs

Figs are highly nutritious and this recipe simply makes it more tempting to eat.

Serving Size: 5-6
Ingredients:

1. 10 **figs** (dried and split)
2. 10 tsp **almond butter**
3. ¼ cup **coconut** (dried and shredded)
4. 10 **whole pecans**

Procedure:
1. In the split figs, pour almond butter and roll in the shredded coconut.
2. Lightly press the whole pecans in and serve.

Lemony Pudding

Lemony Pudding is a refreshing delight especially during the summers. Inclusion of real lemon juice makes this a very alkaline recipe.

Serving Size: 1-2
Ingredients:
1. 2 cups **avocado** (mashed)
2. 1 ½ cups **lemon flesh** (peeled and seeded)
3. 1 **lemon** (juice)
4. 2 cups **dates** (pitted)

Procedure:
1. In a food processor, blend all the ingredients to get a smooth consistency.
2. Refrigerate for an hour and serve.

Blueberries Blast

Blueberries Blast is an interesting dessert for festive occasions that can be prepared quickly.

Serving Size: 2-3
Ingredients:

1. ¼ Cup **blueberries** (pitted)
2. 2 **bananas** (chopped)
3. ½ **lemon** (juice)

Procedure:
1. In a food processor, blend all the ingredients well in a smooth consistency.
2. Refrigerate for about 2-3 hours and serve.

Peach Pie

This peach pie recipe combines healthy nuts and coconut filling to create an alkaline infusion.

Serving Size: 3-4
Ingredients:

Crust
1. 1 cup **almonds** (chopped)
2. 1 cup **dates** (pitted)

Layer
1. 1-2 **peaches** (pitted and chopped)

Filling
1. ¼ cup **coconut** (shredded)
2. ¼ cup **pine nuts** (chopped)
3. 4-5 **peaches** (pitted and chopped)
4. 1 Tsp **lemon** (juice)

Procedure:
1. To prepare the crust, blend dates and almonds. Pour this mix in pie dish and arrange the peaches over it.
2. Blend all the ingredients for filling, and pour it over the pie crust. Refrigerate for about 1-2 hours and serve.

Green Pumpkin Pie

Pumpkin Pie is a popular dessert recipe all across the Western part of the world. This special alkaline pumpkin pie recipe is VERY interesting as we are using avocados, which blend surprisingly well with pumpkin and infuse what would be an ordinary pie with tons of nutrients, omega fatty acids, and alkalinity.

Serving Size: 4-5
Ingredients:

1. 1 cup **raw macadamia nuts** (chopped)
2. 1 cup **organic raisins** (soaked)
3. 4 cups **pumpkin** (peeled and chopped)
4. 2 **avocados** (peeled and seeded)
5. 1 cup **raw honey**
6. 1 **vanilla bean** (soaked for an hour)
7. 1 tsp **cinnamon** (powdered)
8. 1 tsp **nutmeg** (powdered)
9. 1 tsp **ginger** (grated)
10. ½ tsp **sea salt**
11. 1 cup **water**
12. 4-8 tbsp **psyllium husks**

Procedure:
1. Blend all the ingredients in a food processor except pumpkin and psyllium husks. Once the mix is smooth enough add pumpkin and then psyllium husks.
2. Refrigerate it for about 5-6 hours before serving.

Coco-Orange Delight

Coco-Orange Delight combines the unique blend of coconut and orange.

Serving Size: 4-5
Ingredients:

Flan:
1. 2 cups **young coconut meat** (chopped)
2. ¼ cups **dates** (pitted)
3. 2 ½ tsp **vanilla**
4. 1 ½ tsp **psyllium powder**
5. Pinch of **Celtic Sea Salt**
6. ¾ Cup **coconut water**

Glaze:
1. 2 **oranges** (juice)
2. 1 ½ cup **dates** (pitted)
3. ¾ tsp **cinnamon** (powdered)
4. Pinch of **Celtic Sea Salt**
5. 2 tsp **psyllium powder**

Procedure:
1. To prepare flan, blend all the ingredients mentioned. Refrigerate for an hour or so to set.
2. In a blender, combine all the ingredients for glaze.
3. On a serving plate, serve flan along with glaze.

Wholesome Cookie

Buckwheat makes a healthy alternative to regular flour.

Serving Size: 5-6
Ingredients:

1. 2 ½ cups of **sprouted buckwheat groats** (soaked for 8-10 hours)
2. 1 cup **raisins** (soaked 6 hours)
3. 1/4th cup **organic butter**
4. 1 tbsp **vanilla**
5. ½ cup **dark chocolate** (lightly sweetened)

Procedure:
1. In a food processor, blend all the ingredients.
2. Bake it for about 25- 30 minutes and serve.

Date Dazzle

Date Dazzle is based on dates as its main ingredients that are highly nutritious and an instant source of energy.

Serving Size: 6-7
Ingredients:
1. 1 cup **dates** (pitted)
2. 2 Cups **raisins** (pitted and soaked)
3. 2 Cups **currants** (pitted and soaked)
4. 2 Cups **Pecans**
5. 1 **Lemon** (zest)
6. 2 Cups **Filberts** (hazel nuts)
7. 2 Tsp **lemon juice**
8. 1 tsp **lemon rind**

Procedure:
1. Blend nuts and raisins to prepare the bottom layer for the recipe. To prepare lemon date frosting, blend dates and lemon juice along with lemon rind.
2. Scoop and fill the torte with about ½ of the frosting.
3. To make the top layer, blend the remaining layer and cover the torte.
6. Decorate with the remaining frosting.

Yummy Yam

Yummy Yam is an innovative twist to the popular yam.

Serving Size: 4-5
Ingredients:

Almond Date Crust
1. 1 ¼ Cup **almonds** (soaked overnight)
2. 1 Cup **date pieces** (soaked and pitted)
3. 1 Tbsp **water**
4. ½ tsp **vanilla**
5. ¼ Cup **cinnamon** (powdered)
6. 2 tsp **psyllium**

Filling
1. 6 small **medium yams** (peeled and chopped)
2. ⅛ tsp **5 spice powder**
3. ¾ Cup dates (soaked and pitted)
4. ¼ Cup **raisins** (soak for 20 minutes)
5. ½ Cup **Pine Nuts** (soaked 5-10 minutes)
6. ½ tsp **cinnamon** (powdered)
7. ⅛ tsp **Garam masala**
8. ½ tsp **vanilla**
9. 2 Tbsp **Psyllium powder**

Procedure:
1. Blend all the ingredients mentioned for the crust. Press the mix in a pie dish and keep it aside for dehydrating.
2. Prepare the filling by blending all the ingredients, and pour into the crust.
3. Refrigerate it for a few hours to set.

Blissful Vanilla

Blissful Vanilla is a homemade nutritious ice-cream with coconut as its base.

Serving Size: 2-3
Ingredients:

1. 1 ½ cups **young coconut meat**
2. 1 ½ cups **coconut water**
3. ¼ cups **Agave**
4. ½ **lemon** (juice)
5. 3 Tsp **coconut butter**
6. 3-4 tsp **Stevia**
7. 1 tsp **vanilla extract**

Procedure:
1. In a food processor, blend all the ingredients and refrigerate until semi set.
2. Process the blend and refrigerate for a few hours until set.

Fruity Crumble

Fruity Crumble is a fantabulous recipe that lets you enjoy the goodness of fruits and nuts in one.

Serving Size: 4-5
Ingredients:

1. 4 cups **Seasonal fruit** (thinly sliced)
2. ½ cup **raisins** (soaked and pitted)
3. 1 ½ Tsp **cinnamon** (powdered)
4. ½ **lemon** (juice)
5. 1 tsp **nutmeg** (powdered)
6. ½ tsp **Celtic salt**
7. 2 cup **pecans** (soaked 10-12 hours)
8. 1 cup **dates** (pitted and soaked)
9. ¼ Cup **coconut** (shredded)

Procedure:
1. In a blender, combine together seasonal fruit, soaked raisins, lemon juice, cinnamon, and nutmeg as well as Celtic salt.
2. Pour this mix over a sliced seasonal fruits.
3. Blend dates and coconut in a smooth consistency and pour over the other layers.
4. Dehydrate it for 3-5 hours at a temperature of about 110° F.

Delicious Bread Pudding

Delicious Bread Pudding is tasty and super easy to prepare dessert that has been popular for many centuries.

Serving Size: 5-6
Ingredients:

1. 1 loaf **raisin bread.**
2. 4 cups **coconut milk**
3. 4 **organic eggs**
4. ½ cup **coconut palm sugar**
5. 1 tsp **vanilla extract**

Procedure:
1. In a bowl, blend all the ingredients except the bread.
2. Soak the bread slices in the mix and bake in a preheated over at a temperature of about 350° F.

Lemongrass Legacy

Lemongrass Legacy is an easy to prepare dessert that can brighten up a party by this innovative use of something we wouldn't ordinarily think of as a dessert option.

Serving Size: 2-3
Ingredients:

1. **1 large lemongrass stalks**(chopped)
2. 2 cups **water**
3. ¾ Cup **honey**
4. ½ tsp **pure vanilla**
5. ⅓ Cup **chia seeds**
6. 1 Cup **seasonal fruit** (chopped)

Procedure:
1. Pulverize the lemongrass by blending it with water.
2. Blend other ingredients into the lemongrass mix.
3. In this, add the chia seeds and refrigerate for about 20-25 minutes.

Fruit filled Flatbread

Fruit filled flatbread can be a great idea to implement some seasonal fruit into your diet.

Serving Size: 4-5
Ingredients:

1. 4 **apples** (cored and chopped)
2. 1 **Fuji apple** (cored and chopped)
3. 1 ½ cup **ground flax seed**
4. **1 tbsp cinnamon** (powdered)
5. ½ cup **filtered water**
6. 4 tbsp **raw honey**
7. ⅛ tsp **stevia**
8. ¼ Cup **walnuts** (chopped)
9. ¼ tsp **cloves** (crushed)
10. ½ cup **coconut** (flakes)
11. 2 tbsp **coconut oil**

Procedure:
1. In a food processor, blend all the ingredients to get a paste-like consistency.
2. Divide into equal portions and spread on the parchment paper.
3. Dehydrate for 8-10 hours at a temperature of 115° F.

Banana Pie

Banana pie is good healthy dessert that can be prepared quickly. More alkaline goodness with dates and coconut.

Serving Size: 5-6
Ingredients:
Crust:
1. 1 Cup **Almonds**
2. 3-4 tsp **maple syrup**

Filling:
1. 6 **Bananas** (chopped)
2. ½ Cup **dates** (chopped)
3. 1 tsp **vanilla extract**
4. 1 Cup **coconut** (shredded)
5. 2 Tbsp **Coconut** (shredded)

Procedure:
1. To prepare the crust, blend all the ingredients mentioned and press it on a pie tray. Keep some of this mix to cover the pie after filling.
2. Prepare the filling by blending all the ingredients and pour onto the pie crust.
3. Cover the filling with the crust mix and refrigerate for a few hours to set.

Minty Pudding

Minty Pudding is definitely a must try among the alkaline desserts.

Serving Size: 3-4
Ingredients:

1. 2 cups **raw coconut meat**
2. 1 cup **raw unsweetened strained coconut milk**
3. ¼ cup **Natural Mint Flavored Liquid Chlorophyll**
4. ¼ cup **almond butter**
5. 1 Tbsp **chia seeds**
6. 1 tsp **Mint Flavor**
7. 80 drops **Stevia**

Procedure:
1. Blend all the ingredients in a food processor.
2. Refrigerate it for a few hours and serve.

Manic Mousse

Manic Mousse is a low calorie, high alkaline version of the Chocolate Mousse that we all love.

Serving Size: 3-4
Ingredients:

1. 3 **bananas** (chopped)
2. 5 tbsp **cacao powder**
3. ½ **large avocado** (chopped)
4. 2 tbsp **coconut water**
5. ¼ tsp **vanilla extract**
6. 2-5 drops **liquid stevia**

Procedure:
1. Blend all the ingredients into a food processor.
2. Pour it into a dish and refrigerate for a few hours before serving.

Chocolate Pudding

Chocolate Pudding is a universal favorite dessert around the world. Enjoy this imaginative spin on it.

Serving Size: 1-2
Ingredients:

1. ½ medium sized **avocados** (chopped)
1. ¼ tsp **vanilla extract**
2. 1 ½ tbsp **hemp nuts** (chopped)
2. 1 ½ tbsp **cacao powder**
3. 6-8 drops **liquid stevia**
3. 1-2 tsp **agave syrup**
4. pinch of **Celtic sea salt**
5. 5-10 tbsp **coconut milk**

Procedure:
1. Blend all the ingredients into a smooth mix.
2. Pour it into a dish and refrigerate for a few hours.

Final Thoughts

What I did not mention at the beginning of this book is that there are many personal stories I can recall of people healing themselves through balancing their alkalinity. It is hard to report these stories formally because they are simply anecdotes. But, they persist. I could, for instance, talk about my uncle who was diagnosed with a metastatic tumor on his stomach. He was preparing for surgery as well as chemo and radiation. He spent those weeks in-between alkalizing himself as much as possible, with concentrated jalapeno peppers among other recipes. Mysteriously, the cancer disappeared by the time he was ready for surgery.

The skeptics always say these stories are just attributable to chance, but how can we say something is chance when it happens again, and again? It's hard to scientifically test some of these claims, because it's never going to be a totally repeatable and consistent. However, I think the link is definitely there.

Alkalinity could be the key to balancing your body's health. Some of us feel we are predestined to inherit diseases like cancer due to genetics. However, I believe there is hope for all of us, so long as health, vitality and the extension of our mortality for as long as possible are causes we truly care about. So here's to your long-term health, I hope alkalinity will play an important part of it.

A Message from Andrea

Thank you so much for taking the time to read this book. I hope that this was of some benefit to you.

You can find the rest of the books in this series by checking out www.developedlife.com/andreasilver. You can also reach me personally by e-mailing: AndreaSilverWellness@gmail.com.

Free Gift: At the Andrea Silver page on Developed Life, don't forget to sign-up for my free PDF e-book companion, *The 20 Most Deceptive Health Foods*, which will educate you on the dishonest health food brands and the truly healthy alternatives.

Until next time,
Andrea